scarecrow

wesleyan poetry

robert fernandez

SCA
REC
ROW

Wesleyan University Press — Middletown, Connecticut

Wesleyan University Press
Middletown CT 06459
www.wesleyan.edu/wespress
2016 © Robert Fernandez
All rights reserved
Manufactured in the United States of America
Designed by Mindy Basinger Hill
Typeset in Electra LT Standard

Library of Congress Cataloging-in-Publication Data
available upon request.

for mary and for mimi

contents

Scarecrow 1

When for a Moment 3

It Would Be Better If You Tasted Rain 5

We Adorn 7

If I Offend You with My Leniency 8

The Dauphin 9

A Vein of Earth 11

After Antonioni's *La Notte* 12

Pack 15

Lost Time 16

Sing Again 17

Rogue Estates 18

Your Loves Travel and Stand 19

Bantams 20

And 22

So Strange Arrangements 23

All the Deadly Ones 24

The Dog 25

The Ground Beneath 26

The Leaning 27

Flags 28

Full Day 29

Ad Absurdum 30

Bruckner Grew Up among Weevils 31

Dayrun 32

Those You Live Among 33

In Winter with Starred Standards 34

The Blood Desires Nakedness of Every Sort 35

Crowns 36

Then from the Bronze World 37

Vincent 38

Of Listening and Patient Work 39

How Could I Have Clipped So Near 40

They Remember My Name 42

What Tree Does Give 43

We Are Elsewhere 44

Who Makes a Chorus of You Here 46

Tasso 47

Fêtes 48

You Are Not Here 50

We Challenge 52

Where You Hunt, Your Blood Goes Cold 54

Softly the Day Stands 55

I Want to Die Better 57

Which Chatters Beauty 59

Every Horned Wayfarer 61

Thanatos 63

Again 65

—

Acknowledgments 69

scarecrow

scarecrow

Bring your servants close.
Nesting is not a time.
There is no damage here.
The brain is fine. The leaves,
fine. The wine is as black as ever

—

There is a pace
and it slows
and it sees
and it
lows

—

One slickens up to you, all
oil, to assure you of your substance.
This is all all all. Make a note
of it. Herein lies a balance
for yellow birds with black heads
and black moths with yellow heads
and all detritus of coming near
the realm of the dead—namely,
yellow and black leaves softened parting

—

So I am a pairing—I know my rules:
let sheep eat sheep and lions, lions.
Let Latins meet Greeks under patch-
work quilts. Let the vision plaid
for a bit

—

I bit
and the grapefruit had a bit
of death's black and from my tear ducts
came grapefruit seeds, black
as hor-
nets. Pity
them Lord for they know not
what they do. Pity the lions and the locusts

—

Pity the animals—the day is a raze,
heat and wheat gathered into airy combines
of thrashing. The noise spins lions
in the air. My fair one falls
down to me on black ropes. No
one can see me, and hope is a thing
for birds and fools. I drool
on locust bouquets and steps
of honey. Come

—

Meet your master
in the dust; with his
one tooth, he drains
you dry. May you spin
here, scarecrow, among
the other straw-like things
planted in the dark earth,
swollen with light and time

when for a moment

When for a moment
you eat through
the air to swallow
syrupy red letters
Poe
Poe
Poe

—

And bells could be
jasmine and gold,
bone and soap,
seaweed and ivy

—

Crack dread's
red egg on
the burning rock
and let your eyes
speak, your hands
walk

—

The lake
unveils its planks;
you find your way
to the red silk pavilion

—

A meal of steaks and pearls
in impossible heat
with cameras at

—

Every angle
and the lions, too,
with watchful eyes—

—

Drain that bourbon
to the red, to the dre-
gs of silt and baboon,
to all animals mashed
and quiet, disastered
and interred, en-
tered in stasis, in
stillness

it would be better if you tasted rain

It would be better if you tasted rain
than this spiced asphalt,
leavened brown horizon and flapjack
blacktop

—

Pollution gets in the skin, spices it
red brown red yellow red brown,
so we

—

Take a swim beyond the dusty chambers of summer,
out where coasts decant coolness and fins rising
from heat slicks reveal cooler depths

—

If time's a chance to stand outside romance
with the immediacies of never-ending foliage
and mark mark mark yes! our pastures for our own
and forthcoming disasters—

—

Here is a bust that rolls down a hill and breaks the water,
fat with coolness

—

I wanted to know a name; I played sports; I
wore shorts; I had a mother and a father (they did too); I
challenged every bone, went south for the winter; I
ate duck, roasted; I said "quail" (it buoyed in me); I
wanted and I wanted, and I

—

Remained. O Icy water, spilled
like a blade across the neck, I ask
that you do your work, I
am tired and it is hot
and today I
have the energy for almost nothing

we adorn

I ask for the broken ladder to fill my head
for sunstroke, red horns of wheat
for dailiness, let me know particulars
O red horn brightened in my chest,
the hairs are countless, I ask
for lozenges like islands, and the color—
red yellow blue—staining the dark
I ask for daylight, forms noticed, held, cut
down from shadow and trembling, held
for the moon's horn filled with red honey
and for the chance of day, a gamble with red chips

The time is taken, culled, like
fruit the time has darkened, blue,
seven panes of glass crushed into the roots
the time is deadly, a coral snake
and we adorn, we adorn

if i offend you with my leniency

If I offend you with my leniency,
I am like a bird with smoked tendons
roughening the hues, fanning my eyes;
my love is a red die rolling in the void

—

And who whistles the empty
pot that burns in your kitchen?
Everything screams
        pointless and damage
damage d-a-m-a-g-e, I
see a kite stuck in a tree
I see a hand thinning and
portents dissolving like fat

—

I cultivate a certain dying I find it
rare, that is my way; I comb it
with exceeding carefulness from
my nerves, delicately as a kite

—

I am the brown bittered
fig skinned with tomb
leeks in brown sauce
and a winking eye
like a suede curtain

—

and am soles of the feet
gold that clicks
its tongue against the roof
of the mouth *rafraf rafraf*

the dauphin

Sometimes
you have to break him
before he'll ride,

—

Sometimes you have to
braid him
before he'll rye

—

Sometimes a smile sits
in the center of the table
like a rare roast beef

—

And sometimes tragedy is lop-
limbed sometimes plates of spa-
ghetti spaghetti spa-

—

Ghetti and
strawberries
in black bowls;

—

Sometimes
cabbage and
black liver

—

The Dauphin sez "blood in shaved ice!"
or "blood shaved down to
a black carriage!"

—

The vultures *hath*; they are *wroth*;
the ghouls are broad shouldered and recline
comfortably across our stomachs

—

Never never never second-
guess yourself, sez he, whose teeth
shine and brown like butter

a vein of earth

What force in flies? Are you
insistent? Are you dead?
Are you guilty? Has your
name been lifted, a vein
of earth from earth?

Your eyes' marvelous bandaging
in crisp clean bandaging in
bone-dry depth so that the eyes,
uncovered, may see—

—

Unwrap! Plague plague plague
is smeared through the city,
and the heavy-breasted bird retracts
claws over rock

Crowns claw over rock,
Oh how fitting for
broken bottled
blacks and greys

—

Yet sometimes
a dark red snakes
toward sunset,
raising a fine dust

And sometimes punishment is
absolute and sometimes
we are abandoned

after antonioni's *la notte*

The champagne comes
and white stairways fly, jet-black
strawberries and white
stairways fly from
hospital silver. Release the trays
of gold

—

Truffles to the animals—they
claw our suits, mal-
aise ma-
laise m-
a-l-a-i-s-e

—

Into whose marble arms are we
released and what grey veins?
Each rocket is a cairn
of fibrous smoke.
Find your way home.
Find your way back
to me,

—

I know
you'll settle here.
Here, worm touches sky.
Here, glass facades are robust,
fibrous water

—

Stop beside the tracks
for coffee-colored rust—the rust
is everywhere beneath the light.
The boys with the rockets.
They're gone now.
They're gone now.
They
are
gone
now

—

How pretty the pool is
with its blue garlands
on white garlands
with its frayed crowns
with its beetles and leaves

—

How pretty the pool is
with its teething garlands of blue
and its trim-torsoed, long-limbed light

—

When the statues wake,
I cut their cheeks, Ozymandias

—

When the statues wake,
the light and skin align;
briskly the flesh chatters

—

Valentina, seven-pointed star,
is that black blood pooling
in your mouth? Have the lines
around the buzzards' eyes
turned silver? What shall
we play for? When you

—

Were sick, I
came to you; I tended you; I
loved you; I loved you
despite yourself; I helped you
remember your name

—

These mansions push
a horn in my chest. Let
me savor that debt let me
savor that debt let me savor
that debt

—

Say the strands are bright.
Under long lamps, all-flesh in bright strands.
On slick roads, strands from the lamps,
wet hair and shining laughter.
Take me to hereafters
of chains and milk, refusals.
It's like the sadness of a dog

—

Will the syrinx split the head in two?
The lie's trunk rears between its
two giant ears. We are reduced
and from nothing or not nothing
or from one another and without
restraint or brought to nothing
or very nearly ruin and disaster
disaster dis-aster then not
then take things as they come

pack

What better bread?
What hearts are gone
and beaks knock stone?
What avenues unfold?

‒‒‒‒

Straight to roses ward
and marked off in strips like a criminal;
straight to abandoned
with a roll of gauze filling the mouth

‒‒‒‒

Here golden hearts sing
their wolves' temperament;
here streets announce
bright Prussias of hazel eyes
and index toes

—

I soften at the mouth
as they refuse return, full shore.
The patterns are our pack.
The clouds dimple; their shadows see

—

The temperament is another, wolfish,
trailing a gold string. There

—

Are amities where we lock and
unlock and, meeting, part

lost time

Charm branches sleekly-lost-time,
Nativities, where-would-we-be.
Where would we be without

—

Eating white blossoms
in the slop of every death?
Look

—

At the surface—
a pearly glaze deflects,
yet the eye

—

Loves to wander. Present yourself
in the full radiance of captivation.
Your surface skin drains

—

To zeros. Take your time,
rest assured, we have courage
and genius—thick, cream-

—

Colored leaves. Evening is a mess
of blond radials and alliance sings of love,
of show-us-the-bare-neck, of the fig tree

—

And where we are. Where we are is ships
crossing the rich dark and slits-of-
the-eye rudders

sing again

Westron wynde sweeps hooks toward
what is held. Nothing's held

Nothing's meat buckles and
the moon rises. Nothing's fried

The black lake, cormorant's shine,
the diving board, white foam,

then nothing's splash. Nothing
at the window in Japanese beetles . . .

Nothing nothing nothing
and a soft, red bow. Nothing

on the table with the light.
Nothing and joyful splendor,

black foam. Nothing's eye
and this tall head of straw

in a dead season

rogue estates

Rest of peace. And rogue estates.
Rest of peace where wells blacken.
Rogue estates
      dominos fall to table chatter.
At some streetlight, a fountain,
no names for us homes for us
here, no meals
no medicines for what we missed.
Part of the crane's beak and light's
leech. Step out from the light
into plumper hearts

your loves travel and stand

Still day falls
and love's ghouls
streak the plane.
The heart swallows.
Clip

—

Desire at its root.
Let love stand. Panic
unbraids across the trees
and leaves crossing roofs

—

Your head can't turn
from left to right; the entire
world unwraps beside you. You
are young; your loves
travel and stand. Your time
is homeless

—

When you are hushed, o weapon,
you scrape reduction's black jelly;
when you despair, o gods,
you lead us to war

—

The work dies.
The sun arcs.
Still the rainbow
indicates

—

An absolute desire

bantams

And it is all I have,
this wrinkled duct
pity for which burns
only lightly, a bit of stick
of tree's sap, on the
tongue

—

Would take a blotter
and see the sun's
black dolmen itch
down each of its
four faces, would
know tragedy
and absurdity
like heads packed
in cabbage leaves
what to do
Oh what to do

—

When we
get closer
when the
ring is right
there is a light
bent against black plates
like black linen drapes
stitched from sea
to sun
to sky

—

Breathe a moment
of your silence meat,
sayeth the world, and I
will cut a gash so deep
splendor will show her neck,
rushing up from the dark earth
O rims of scalloped fountains

—

And there to find
there to find there to find
power's
drooping pupil,
heavy-lidded disdain
ma mère grapples by the mane
and would open the vein but
drags us off into the dirt

—

Everything is dust here
and violence and without
the resonance what the fuck

—

Is there to say

and

Give us water and food to pursue our tasks.
Help us not become wards of the state,
impoverished, homeless, destitute, crushed
under the heel, buried in systems, imprisoned,
dead, hospitalized. We die die die. Our dogs
will not walk themselves after we go. Our bodies
will not burn themselves after we go. Our apartments
will not pack themselves after we go. Instead,
bright ribbons of work, tangled in our bodies,
will be vomited out and indeed bright ribbons
will be vomited out. In the meantime,
the light's eyelashes open and close.
And in the meantime, work and reprieve.
Lie down; don't lie; lie flat; lie still. See these
books bound in itching white leather? They are
your life. And each feathery page, lifted by hot wind.
O summer air, o gardens, o seasons o châteaux.
The glaring day, it binds, o occurrence, o soil o soul.

so strange arrangements

So strange arrangements stamped
with Valentines where the red is pure,
and sundown's thousand pillows
are an access of forgetting

—

An access of forgetting,
love takes you, arm in arm;
the entire city goes barefoot
across sundown's red mirrors

—

Where are the clouds
leaner? And a thousand faces greet us
without a single prayer. And to yield
is yielding to Abelards of forgetting

—

Where the brick is eaten by cloud,
Where are the pears white?
Where are the pears white?
Where are the pears white?

all the deadly ones

We want you to kill us, our

—

Time has run thin, let the young with bloodlust in their
mouths, watering their mouths, come to interview us, who
are fresh game, where

—

The water seems sunken, a storage unit of brown boxes, we
will sit, under hot lights, spilling tokens from our heads, ready
to burn like summer shuckings, white ears of corn white ears
of corn

—

Who then will release us? Who
then will

—

Release
us?

—

I had a tower, it was many-hued, it played the world, it played
the game, it followed its name into transience and death, o
crushed horn, where are you now, dripping
streaked maize along the streets
death is an answer, stop

—

Filling us with such slop, poète
maudit ain't got a drop to sell
and wears yellow and orange
striped socks, dancing on hell's
zebra mirror

the dog

is huge as a roll
of industrial rug, stretched
to fill the 77th floor of a high-rise
in Manhattan

—

The dog's heart
is connected to a spine,
a flight of bone steps
extending down to a stomach,
taut and empty

—

The emptiness of the stomach
makes a paltry music, pulsing
and twinkling with repressions,
a swelling as the long cavities
of muscle flush, pull, and bend

—

The dog tabulates,
a hand nonchalantly tallying
at an abacus drenched in saliva and foam

—

The pink and black gums
conceal the gold tooth of an infinite, irrepressible
failure of savor

the ground beneath

Can I get at your knots?
Will your slits have me?
Who says your armpits are full of folds?
And your wrists, colored paper?
And under your tongue, colored paper?

Will you bring me back to myself?
Was I hard to find, rolling in saltwater?
Did you feel my burden, two buckets
full of clay? Didn't you want to shrug it off
for a moment?

Wasn't this summer, season of rest?
Were the dead restless in the tall trees?
Were the young bright in summer's doorways?
Did the water burn brightly in its jugs?

Where was anyone to help us?
Where were our fathers and our sisters?
O my friends, o my love, we were ours,
where was the breath and ground beneath us?

the leaning

Was the pleasure of the air I took
like rope ladders like fountains I
could tell you of leaping animals
leaping to their deaths I could tell
of formative deaths that led to
leaping I could tell of monsters
pinned with ribbons and the face clean
as the body of a wasp and taking
the pleasure of the air I could tell
of fortresses covetousness and care
I could tell, too, of divestments, of
I-am-not-ours, of we-are-not-theirs
and of raw linen pinned with hours
and skin shining with sweat I could
tell of the work done here on our behalf
how it smiles I could tell of the water-
wheel's laughing and the flags' laughing
and of the hope of not seeing I am the bend
in the road that cuts the burden in half
I am the avenue that dies in jubilee
I take the pleasure of the air in tresses
there are storms up ahead I take the water
I take the fountain in my mouth I take
the way

flags

Choose a flag,
one that itches, raw
glass, and draw it close

—

Comfort is for those
whose eyes can shut but
all wallets close at once, all eyes

—

All hands all hearts, blood
chambers—no-
thing speaks,
in the vast hall nothing speaks,
the air conditioner blows and the glass
tomb's color is perfect

—

I would bend you toward speed of day you
are not yet aligned you
are too slow slow slow or or or
you're not quite yes yes yes and must
align perfectly with break of day,
unwrapping inch by inch of stubborn canvas
to winds that would clean their teeth on you

—

So the day is murder;
still there's a bit, here and there, to say to day—
say ears are enfolded listening, colored flags, yes
again say nothing and no one
is ever enough there is no time yes yes never sorrow
never enough

full day

Time to lend you an apple, o
Marianne, so you can eat the season
straight off

—

Break for me just a bit, at the knee,
let it roughen from your voice
say what there is to see
tell us what's in front of you

—

your stomach holds the dice
your blood's a weather vane
your head's an untidy box

—

What miracle everything's soft and bends for you
be happy today is full day, saturated
nothing else be happy, your loved ones care for you
be happy, the light shines on you be happy
you are in your body, a great boat on seas of flesh
and of work, be happy
be happy
be happy

ad absurdum

I call tricks
because I don't have enough for a lung
or a heart or a shard of black bowel
so who are you to fling chips, remain

—

The desert dweller, tenant of dry places, I like
the gold tooth tucked into your skull
and the ravenous wool tooth
tucked into your skull and the Nile of leather
tucked into your skull

—

Fix me a raiment of days, I wait
for your shuckings of heat, your turn, I await
your motive, a dog's gums drawn down, tongue revealed,
I refuse to dream anymore, heat gathers around
my teeth, I am close to speech's refusal pour
some water from your horn along my ribs, can't

—

You see that the days are exhausted, that we
move from island to island, that we will be left
to be picked at by gold birds?

—

Who flings meat at you to continue
who has your best interests in mind who loves you
who lends you time who worries about your health?

—

There is a chorus of burdens that would restore
you to the earth but the fountains' brilliant black
holds those birds delicately at the rims and they
very nearly dissolve in the light and what they
sing anyway is abrasion

bruckner grew up among weevils

Will you consider my standing?
Bruckner grew up among weevils

—

Where, when do I stand?
Not him not her not this but that
not opened and so closed.

I work and in my chest
a typewriter ball spins its horizontal eye,
leaky and smearing horizons

—

My pleasure is the game and love of summer.
Let there be games tonight and studded answers,
bistros and men with red shins.

Let Sin's ladders climb to leafy heights.

Our stomachs grin.
The table spins

like something called
confetti or "carefree." To-

—

day day day the Drs. smile at me, much
to their (and my) surprise. And at evening, brown
sugar cones and a walk through the park, a red
Comme des Garçons heart
on my sneakers

dayrun

Then time to crack the trunk
and spill diamonds, yellow yellow
yellow the worst is near the worst
is here snapping at
the foot of the bed

—

You
have been reduced,
Kierkegaard and Heidegger in the dayroom
overlooking your friend's
professorate, chatting with Isaiah

—

Say
you have been mawed, sealed
rooms, laptops and observation,
tell the court, tell the court, tell
the court the prodigal is
star-stitched

—

A waterfall spills at his neck,
crystals crust, wintry, the side
of his chest, there
is something speaking
along solid faces, gather

—

Me toward gather me toward
gather me toward there is a tower
between my index finger and middle finger it
is delicate as paper and sucks up ash
and bores a soul in my temple

those you live among

I have no camera
no game no tent, no word no mon-
strance no belt, no vent no succor,
no assuage no guilt, no music

—

The boarders they play games with you
those whose stomachs are full
of steaks they toy with you, the house
is full of toys

—

And each day, crime is easier, those
I live among, those I live among let me have my
speech, I can
not speak rocks in oil flounder
in oil and window pane almond al-
mond who is fragrant enough to live
among? Who is fair enough to be set beside?

—

My days are broken
and setting
and more truthful

—

The light despises me food
despises me the word despises me
I am no fate
I am no fate-in-his-robes
no styled light today I am bled
I see the rainbow's metal blinds open
I am time, purple gold dripping out, sail-
fish fans monstrance monstrance
monstrance
　　I am no ointment here
　　　I am no bruise-paste-of-day

in winter with starred standards

In winter with starred standards
behind which the sun flows
In winter with starred standards
behind which the sun flows
In winter with starred standards
behind which the sun flows

—

I have no horns, I cannot molt and
leave you horns, I have
no horns yet from the curled
lead you draw off milk
I have no horns for you you you
the gold in withered horns you you you

—

O my love you you you
and the shelf in your chest is marble
and the heart that burns there, red velvet
and the flame that knots, clear
and the water that drips, blackest
and the music the music the music

the blood desires nakedness of every sort

What nude will take you soon,
if not by the wrist then by snaring
the hook of your open collar; noon
desires nakedness of every sort

—

The blood
desires nakedness of every sort,
as at city hall, faces freeze,
nearly a hundred watchful faces freeze
and stare, and under your checkerboard jacket
you, a child, are a surge of blood among children

—

The windows are kites but we cut
their throats first; the vultures settle
on window frames window
frames window
frames

—

The meal's a bowl of pastel-colored
potatoes; with every slice their color
bleeds and unravels rings that are
undone

—

Mothers among us,
examine your hands; a serpent
kisses the palms with a light
flick of the tongue

—

No hell-of-disdain has poured
its pastel concrete; still, bitter rinds
of twilight stagger down our backs

crowns

One gathers and spends
some night. Some night

reaches up in flutes of
oranges and becomes

some night. A licorice
of tongues licks from the

chandelier. The bridge
to joy is treacherous.

Where is the harvest,
where the meal? Our

cousins find our names
too sweet, our meat too

sweet, our sweat too c-r-
o-w, too c-r-o-w-n, our

necks too much like c-r-
o-w-n-s. O forked alliance

blessed with droplet red
and fever, we are citizens

of the world, and of sun

then from the bronze world

Then from the bronze world
fountains and caves,
brown roses bent
to peaks of bone, beaks

—

Knock
on the glitter of fountains.
Should it be blood
if we are eating

—

Sweat, and honey cakes
blister what we arrest
of thought, sun's
mess of red spaghetti?

—

Messes call down
crows which enter the blood
and draw their beaks
through bloody strands, we

—

Did not serpent,
did not suspect
we were being
nudged clean

vincent

Vincent,
it's where the beading
stops and

—

Vincent,
it's where the beading
stops

—

Vincent,
it's where the beading stops
and the blood drains into a bowl

—

Vincent,
only our loves
come to drink

—

Vincent,
the yellows and reds
are crystal

—

Vincent,
the yellows and blues
drift through the horn of the head

—

Vincent,
the sun's sagging eye
drops toys on us

of listening and patient work

I hold
the work
I
was nursed I
was shuttled
I lost my name
I could not see
I could not see debt
I could not see love
I could not see sickness
or health or ruin
I could not see
O draft of lilies
I am delivered
I and grace
I
am ashamed
I am humbled
I ruin and I
reprieve
I witness love

how could i have clipped so near

Rhododendrons craft
a coat of many colors
for sun the color
of rhododendrons

—

The pile of rhododendrons
we eat when the stomach
is rhododendron glass, hunger

—

Is curved
like a barnacle,
grips

—

The past and its silk
of ruins, no
rhododendron silk,

—

No pier
on which
love stands
overlooking

—

A rhododendron-glass sea—how
could I have clipped so near
to ruin

—

How could love have stood
so fast, I
know debt
but that is not need, no
rhododendron-colored bills

—

To elaborate our foreignness,
to elaborate forgiveness

they remember my name

Under the rain that pulls the gods by their baby-black
hair.—They remember my name, I
remember my name. How

—

Did a name stoop so forcefully
under coal-black shores, crayon-black
shores—we chart through mud,

—

We plod, we
cut through earth,
we are born

—

Through earth,
and bitter crops stoop
to bear the burden lightly, love

—

A black crayon scrawls the light

what tree does give

What tree does give
of its burden in plates even
sliding all of a sun all all all of a sun
all of a sudden from the truck bed
to the asphalt in sheets of glassy so-
und sound sound?

—

Everything crashes, every-
thing's a mane beneath which flesh
flexes, and what's your burden have
you lost your hair what's your sour
what makes your stomach a withery
pit? Tell me

—

Truly and I'll release you—I want no
simple days; rather, I want forms cut
like hours to each precise transient hue.
Never ever land eat sand burn in the skillet

—

Grease and lard grease and lard
the day is hard

—

Is a black lava bed covered with flamingos
that rise in unison

we are elsewhere

Let them
be torn
by

—

Dogs, by buds,
by odes
to joy

—

This is no surety
but to glide the rift,
we feel grateful

—

For sanity
for the press
of talk
for care

—

It comes
like a miracle, we

—

Feel grateful
For   reprieve
     reprieve
     reprieve

—

The day
is wrapped
in silver paper

—

We
are elsewhere

in shadow
in the bleeding
sinuses of ruins, the day's

reprieve
is finely spotted

—

She lyre she can attest
she lyre but lets
the wheel
claw out

—

We stand
as tall as wheat,
as wheel's thin strands
of lights, we break
from spoked centers

who makes a chorus of you here

Really I am leaving you the point
point which is hard meat, bone, stone
and the flint that brings the forehead bone
to flame, we

—

Work hard, we are tools, we
are relevant singulars scraping stone, shuttling
ash, say

—

You'd rather have a song from us, scraping ash, I
prefer the dashboard wet with evening and our
bodies turning, bodies turned—like the poem,
master, windowpane window pane window p-
a-n-e

—

Quietly to our succor, window, quietly to our succor
"danger lurks around every corner"
daylight lurks around every corner, a man
in block-velour suit, a ziggurat, head stretched
to the tops of the buildings

—

Who makes a chorus of you here,
let's bring him colorful fruits and flowers,
every stanching of colorful flowers to fill the wells
and wounds, garlands of fruit-colored silvery flowers
for necks and heads and thighs and arms and wrists, help
us purveyors of mystery bring beauty to the brown dust form
of day, let us

—

Feast a while, for we have the time

tasso

In the madhouse of St. Anna,
we cover the knees with blood beads
where the depth of our pleading for Silvias
is like black leaves drawn up
in endless buckets from a well

—

Children bring their buckets to the shore,
green and yellow, green and yellow as in
the madhouse of St. Anna we boil sand
dollars and watch ladders and jets stretch
into the thrashings of tree tops

—

Nothing you could have done would have borne
you right. For twenty years, misery and sickness
slipped their mask between your shoulder blades
and burdened you with contours and with eyes
fixed rigidly toward the earth

—

Bring your carriage to Sant'Onofrio where dark
jets will issue from you, will stiffen to blinding pillars
and the dogs will sport beneath you and the winds
tangle beneath you and the fountains
laugh beneath you

fêtes

Green barges
fill the night
and green clouds

—

Fill the night
and the lime trees
fatten with night

—

On the barges,
the night's drawn up
into chandeliers—

—

The mosquitos, cool
and smooth and cut
from coal, illuminate

—

Feasting.
The skin is naked
as a die;

—

The drone
of mosquitos rolls
from our talk;

—

Green dresses
issue a pink mist
and mouths roll over

—

Bars of coal, a smooth
speech of the dead.
The barges and their

—

Chandeliers lift
into the leaves
of lime trees,

—

Into strands
of starlight

you are not here

You are not here.
The eyes dilate
and coasts harden to green-
blue waters and
      boardwalks
      boardwalks
      boardwalks

—

I make a mansion
of this house. Some simple
dying happens in the rooms.
A horn flowers on the couch

—

Left for a time
where the earth bears us up—
O hardened season
where the earth bears us up.
O cities of forms and cares,
the distances bear us up

—

When in some season
we worked and struggled back,
diamonds and cravats
and sharper angles split the blood

—

Here was the time to be
ravenous. A farther horizon
ate the blood in great drips

—

The blood comes with love
in spoonfuls. It is impossible
to speak

we challenge

We challenge
the skins of the air
to lay their coffins
of summer light—

—

None of us here
with braided
A-frames of summer light
and coal at our tongues
can stretch to speak

—

The plain foreground
is summer. Summer
is dead and thunder.
Summer is a cleft and
distant. They

—

Sheared my shoulders.
They trimmed
my heart. I no longer
know I

—

No longer know
I

—

No longer know

—

I remember she
is there and we
stand the light

—

The elevator, hanging
a single bare
bulb

—

The time wilts.
The folds rot.
The folds fall
and bleed for
all accounts, en-
counters

where you hunt, your blood goes cold

Your loves take on
a harrowing significance,
bright stars of blood
born in bathtubs of ice

—

Let there be bowls
of rice tonight and steam
for naked shoulders; huddle
up among friends, close the door

—

The distance
rattles its horns
and the wheat stands shrill

—

We have the song
from the lady we have
only so much only so much
we have only so much

softly the day stands

Jackson
Pollock
called me
on the sea-
shell foam
and told me
Blue Poles
sold for two
million

—

Where the two million
blue sand dollars
pad the sky,
the clouds crease,
waves flex,
and stars
darken

—

May the dead
harden into
cold candy

—

Softly
the sea sees
me

Softly
the day stands
and strays

—

Mary the dread
hardens into
cold candles—

Seawater folding
in the cuffs,
gold folding
at the drain

—

A serpent
coldly at the drain
and a grainy disc
of sun

—

A weight
of blue sky
and a black slit
of melon

i want to die better

My god, I want
to die better
than I can
and want to carry
names

—

I was taught to believe
that I could eat the ground
and was a singer
and the seeds they pour
like humanness
and the song
it forgets

—

They are not songs
they are going
to kill me I have
a pigeon's feather
in my tongue I
have a print of pigeon's
foot in my brain

—

I was lost
but the summer rolled
me in its wave
I

—

Love her

—

The song goes
cold, braided
Baudelaire bubbles
off the beach in

—

Montauk,
his bobbing head, we
blow smoke in his direction
—*allay allay allay*—

which chatters beauty

Let them be known
to be found,
glacial ear
of corn breaking
from a white sleeve

—

The brain is tough
and leaves today
on a ship that's off
to sink; ex-
cellence!

—

And to sink is off—
pink billiards,
crocodile mouths,
and cakes

—

Stand
where the water's
black as tar,
where the stars
twist to cadences,
where rhythm sets us
in a straw
vest

—

The night
is cherry syrup
and suffocating orcas,
a cosmos of limbs, bright
and brittle, bright
hysterias of eyes, let

—

Your altitudes collapse
and shores restore
to the face, which
chatters beauty

every horned wayfarer

Every horned wayfarer,
every ankh, every
shoulder blade
stretching out
beyond

—

Itself, horizon.
And again the day
is thinning

—

Blond
and knows

—

Itself,
droplets; and
knows itself,
the mirrors spread
unevenly; and
knows the silk
is spread

—

To the mouth's
rotted
corners. He set
a chair
to take in
sea sea sea,
a mighty peeling mottle
of clouds'
distant roughening,
silence and

—

Stony
surface. Let us
look. The room
is full of light. The
answer:
let it take us

thanatos

I had known and understood
the time was near.
The blackboard
cracked. Thunder
fell

—

In red,
and naked faces
roamed the walk.
The sun came through.
Rimbaud's leg again;
he begged. But worms
turned up through the grass,
and purple

—

Flowers. Not
again. Tra-
gedy, and wells.
Wells, wells, wells. Fresh
water, cold, and that wet
wood. Under

—

The umbrella trees
with black wine black
plums black folds, body's
sweater, loose skin, snake
skin, skim the top, black-
er, of our center, ever
colder, suck

—

Suck suck
we draw
it up, draw
the cold, the cold
is ours, we stay the cold,
the cold is

—

Ours, the clod
is ours, the bloc is ours, the
black is ours, the cake is ours,
the star is ours, the lake
is ours, the streak is ours,
the streak of cold, the lock,
the streak of cold, held
cold, held stark, in-
ward

again

Thirty-four, and
death has me eating
out of

—

A vanilla-paper
envelope

—

All the
horrors
of the Mirror, all
of the Have-Not
and Will-Agains

—

But time she spins
with me and each
she stands with me
each there each
each and shall we

—

Really
be gone

—

But for today
and now and pulled
back from the abyss
and the silver
clouds all come
with coils like
dog brains we
still all

—

Travel
we still all
through,
we still all
lightly and
through the night,
through morning,
again again again,
array again, arrayed
again, through
mourning

acknowledgments

Some of these poems were originally published in *Web Conjunctions* and as part of the Poetry Foundation's Poetrynow series. My thanks to the editors.

Special thanks to Suzanna Tamminen for her support of this work.

Thanks to Mary Hickman and Anthony Madrid for their careful readings of early drafts of these poems.

This book would not have been possible without the efforts of Will Aviles, Blake Bronson-Bartlett, Julie Bower, Peter Gizzi, Mary Hickman, Joan James, Bill Jurma, Luke Marshall, Shaun Padgett, Robyn Schiff, Marguerite Tassi, and Nick Twemlow. My thanks to all.

about the author

Robert Fernandez is the author of the poetry collections *We Are Pharaoh* (2011) and *Pink Reef* (2013). His poems have appeared in *Boston Review, Conjunctions, The New Republic, Poetry, A Public Space,* and elsewhere. He was selected as a New American Poet by the Poetry Society of America, and has received a Gertrude Stein Award for Innovative Poetry and a grant from the Andrew W. Mellon Foundation. He is cotranslator of *Azure: Poems and Selections from the "Livre"* (2015).

An online reader's companion is available at robertfernandezsite.wesleyan.edu.